QuEST

Vol 3

Spiritual Thoughts and Talk Starters

By

Jeff Cheney

QuEST

Vol 3

What is a QUEST?

Several years ago, as our children were young, they were assigned to give talks and spiritual thoughts. As we live in a small Branch of The Church of Jesus Christ of Latter-day Saints, this opportunity came very often.

One day our oldest daughter asked my wife what she needed to put into her talk. What she was looking for was the minimum. What did she have to put in to consider it a complete talk.

My wife is one of the brightest people on the face of the earth; she was also an elementary teacher and a seminary teacher at that time, so she was not going to be fooled into giving an easy answer to my daughter. The answer that she gave, however, became a standard in our home and is the basis for this book. She told her that for her talk, and every talk, she needed to have a quote, an experience or story, a scripture and a testimony. We shortened this into Quest.

QU ote

E xperience

S cripture

T estimony

Many years later, we had six missionaries serving from our Branch in many parts of the world. These six included our youngest son, Drew. Because this was such a special time for our Branch, I wanted to do something special for these missionaries. I decided that while they were serving, I would send them a spiritual thought every week in the form of a Quest. As a result, these quests were started.

I have continued to create them and send them, every week, to my nieces and nephews who are serving missions, as well as any missionaries serving from our Branch.

I just thought I would share them with you. I hope they are useful for those times when you need a spiritual thought or a start for a talk.

~Jeff Cheney

Table of Contents

Quest #61
Repentance

Quote:
"Without repentance, there is no real progress or improvement in life. ... Only through repentance do we gain access to the atoning grace of Jesus Christ and salvation. Repentance ... points us to freedom, confidence, and peace."

~ Elder D. Todd Christofferson   October 2011

Experience:
"My soul was harrowed up to the greatest degree and racked with all my sins.

"Yea, I did remember all my sins and iniquities, for which I was tormented with the pains of hell; yea, I saw that I had rebelled against my God, and that I had not kept his holy commandments.

"... So great had been my iniquities, that the very thought of coming into the presence of my God did rack my soul with inexpressible horror.

"... It came to pass that as I was ... harrowed up by the memory of my many sins, behold, I remembered also to have heard my father prophesy ... concerning the coming of one Jesus Christ, a Son of God, to atone for the sins of the world.

"Now, as my mind caught hold upon this thought, I cried within my heart: O Jesus, thou Son of God, have mercy on me. ...

"And now, behold, when I thought this, I could remember my pains no more. ...

"And oh, what joy, and what marvelous light I did behold; yea, my soul was filled with joy as exceeding as was my pain!

"... There can be nothing so exquisite and sweet as was my joy"

~ Alma 36:12–14, 17–21

Scripture:
"Therefore I command you to repent—repent, lest I smite you by the rod of my mouth, and by my wrath, and by my anger, and your sufferings be sore—how sore you know not, how exquisite you know not, yea, how hard to bear you know not.

For behold, I, God, have suffered these things for all, that they might not suffer if they would repent;

But if they would not repent they must suffer even as I;

Which suffering caused myself, even God, the greatest of all, to tremble because of pain, and to bleed at every pore, and to suffer both body and spirit—and would that I might not drink the bitter cup, and shrink—

Nevertheless, glory be to the Father, and I partook and finished my preparations unto the children of men."
~Doctrine and Covenants 19:15-19

Testimony:

"I invite you to feel more joy in your life: joy in the knowledge that the Atonement of Jesus Christ is real; joy in the Savior's ability, willingness, and desire to forgive; and joy in choosing to repent. Let us follow the instruction to "with joy … draw water out of the wells of salvation." May we choose to repent, forsake our sins, and turn our hearts and wills around to follow our Savior. I testify of His living reality. I am a witness and repeated recipient of His incomparable compassion, mercy, and love. I pray that the redeeming blessings of His Atonement may be yours now— and again and again and again throughout your lives, as they have been in mine. In the name of Jesus Christ, amen."
~ By Elder Dale G. Renlund   October 2016

Quest #62
Worth of Souls

Quote:
"This is a paradox of man: compared to God, man is nothing; yet we are everything to God. While against the backdrop of infinite creation we may appear to be nothing, we have a spark of eternal fire burning within our breast. We have the incomprehensible promise of exaltation—worlds without end—within our grasp. And it is God's great desire to help us reach it."
~Dieter F. Uchtdorf   October 2011

Experience:
"Renu, the first of five sisters to join the Church, shared these thoughts:

"Before I started investigating the Church, I didn't really feel that I was very special. I was just one of many people, and my society and culture didn't really teach me that I had any value as an individual. When I learned the gospel and learned that I was a daughter of our Heavenly Father, it changed me. Suddenly I felt so special—God had actually created me and had created my soul and my life with value and purpose.

"Before I had the gospel in my life, I was always trying to prove to others that I was someone special. But when I learned the truth, that I am a daughter of God, I didn't have to prove anything to anyone. I knew that I was special. … Don't ever think that you are nothing."
~ Joy D. Jones   October 2017

Scripture:
"Remember the worth of souls is great in the sight of God;"
~Doctrine and Covenants 18:10

Testimony:
"I have a testimony in my heart, brothers and sisters, that God, our Heavenly Father, and Jesus Christ know and love us individually. I'm not sure I fully understand how, I just know and have experienced that They do. I urge all of us in our own ministries, to our families and to our fellowman, to embrace the Savior's warm invitation to come unto Him, one by one, and be perfected in Him.
I share this witness and hope, in the name of Jesus Christ, amen.
~Elder Ronald A. Rasband   October 2000

Quest #63
The Light of Christ

Quote:

"If you open your mind and heart to receive the Light of Christ and humbly follow the Savior, you will
receive more light. Line upon line, here a little and there a little, you will gather more light and truth into your souls until darkness has been banished from your life."

~ *President Dieter F. Uchtdorf   October 2017*

Experience:

"Nearly a century ago, a family from Oregon was vacationing in Indiana—over 2,000 miles (3,200 km) away—when they lost their beloved dog, Bobbie. The frantic family searched for the dog everywhere but to no avail. Bobbie could not be found.

Heartbroken, they made the trip home, each mile taking them farther away from their cherished pet.

Six months later, the family was stunned to find Bobbie on their doorstep in Oregon. "Mangy, scrawny, feet worn to the bone—[he] appeared to have walked the entire distance … by himself." Bobbie's story captured the imagination of people across the United States, and he became known as Bobbie the Wonder Dog.

Bobbie is not the only animal who has baffled scientists with an amazing sense of direction and instinct for home. Some monarch butterfly populations migrate 3,000 miles (4,800 km) each year to climes better suited for their survival. Leatherback turtles travel across the Pacific Ocean from Indonesia to the coasts of California. Humpback whales swim from the cold waters of the North and South Poles toward the equator and back. Perhaps even more incredibly, the arctic tern flies from the Arctic Circle to Antarctica and back every year, some 60,000 miles (97,000 km).

When scientists study this fascinating behavior, they ask questions such as "How do they know where to go?" and "How does each successive generation learn this behavior?"

When I read of this powerful instinct in animals, I can't help but wonder, "Is it possible that human beings have a similar yearning—an inner guidance system, if you will—that draws them to their heavenly home?"

~ *President Dieter F. Uchtdorf   October 2017*

Scripture:

"Then spake Jesus again unto them, saying, I am the light of the world: he that followeth me shall not walk in darkness, but shall have the light of life."

~John 8:12

Testimony:

"If we both live and proclaim these principles, we will be following Jesus Christ, who is the true Light of the World. We can be a force for righteousness in preparing for the Second Coming of our Lord and Savior, Jesus Christ. We look forward to that beautiful day when "free hearts will sing when the lights go on again all over the world." In the sacred name of Jesus Christ, amen."

~ Elder Quentin L. Cook   October 2010

Quest #64
The Plan of Salvation

Quote:

"As spirit children of God, in an existence prior to mortality, we desired a destiny of eternal life but had progressed as far as we could without a mortal experience in a physical body. To provide that opportunity, our Heavenly Father presided over the Creation of this world, where, deprived of our memory of what preceded our mortal birth, we could prove our willingness to keep His commandments and experience and grow through the other challenges of mortal life. But in the course of that mortal experience, and as a result of the Fall of our first parents, we would suffer spiritual death by being cut off from the presence of God, be soiled by sin, and become subject to physical death. The Father's plan anticipated and provided ways to overcome all of those barriers.
~*Elder Dallin H. Oaks   April 2017*

"Eternal life is not a name that has reference only to the unending duration of a future life; immortality is to live forever in the resurrected state, and by the grace of God all men will gain this unending continuance of life. But only those who obey the fulness of the gospel law will inherit eternal life. ... It is 'the greatest of all the gifts of God ..., for it is the kind, status, type, and quality of life that God himself enjoys. Thus those who gain eternal life receive exaltation; they are sons of God, joint-heirs with Christ, members of the Church of the Firstborn; they overcome all things, have all power, and receive the fulness of the Father."
~*Elder Bruce R. McConkie   Mormon Doctrine, 2nd ed., pg. 237*

Experience:

"A few years ago, right before Christmas, I had a stake conference assignment in California. On the flight back to Utah, I decided to take a short nap. My seat was C, near the aisle. Just before the cabin door closed, a beautiful lady in her mid-70s stood beside me and said, "May I have my seat?" I said, "Yes, ma'am." That was the end of my nap. She loved to talk.

She said, "I don't know why I should have to fly to a cold place like Utah at Christmastime to visit my grandchildren. I hate to leave sunny California."

She went on to say, "Besides, there are strange and weird people in Utah. They call themselves 'Mormons.' My daughter married one of them."

I said, "I am sorry, but before you go any further, I should tell you that I am one of them."

Then she said, "I am sorry—I didn't mean that."

I said, "Oh, you really meant that, didn't you?"

Our conversation went on until we were above Provo. We knew we would soon be landing in Salt Lake.

"Patti"—that's her name—"you have been talking for most of the flight. I feel like I have known you from the pre-earth life. Before we land in Salt Lake City, I'd like to ask you a few questions if I may."

I asked her sincerely, "Patti, your deceased husband—do you know you can see him again?"

She said, "Oh, is that possible?"

"Do you know your deceased son, Matt, who died as a baby—you will see him also in the future?"

Her eyes became moist, and her voice was shaking. The Spirit of the Lord touched her. I sensed she had missed them so much.

Then I prayerfully asked her, "Patti, do you know you have a loving and kind Heavenly Father, who loves you so dearly?"

She said, "Do I?"

"Patti, do you know your Heavenly Father has a special plan for you and that your family can be forever?"

"Can we?" she replied.

"Have you ever heard the plan before?"

She said, "No."

Very sincerely I asked her, "Would you like to know about it?"

"Yes, I would," she responded.

The Spirit of the Lord touched her deeply. And the Lord promises us, "For mine elect hear my voice and harden not their hearts."

He also said: "I am the good shepherd, and know my sheep. ... My sheep hear my voice, and I know them, and they follow me."

~*Elder Yoshihiko Kikuchi*   April 2000

Scripture:

"For behold, this is my work and my glory—to bring to pass the immortality and eternal life of man."

~*Moses 1:39*

Testimony:

"Our beloved Father simply asks that we live by the truth we have received and that we follow the path He has provided. Therefore, let us take courage and trust in the guidance of the Spirit. Let us in word and in deed share with our fellowmen the amazing and awe-inspiring message of God's plan of happiness. May our motive be our love for God and for His children, for they are our brothers and sisters. This is the beginning of what we can do in return for so much.

Someday "every knee shall bow, and every tongue confess" that God's ways are just and His plan is perfect. For you and me, let that day be today. Let us proclaim, with Jacob of old, "O how great the plan of our God!"

Of this I testify in deep gratitude to our Heavenly Father, as I leave you my blessing, in the name of Jesus Christ, amen."

~*President Dieter F. Uchtdorf   October 2016*

Quest #65
Testimony of The Restoration

Quote:

"We believe The Church of Jesus Christ of Latter-day Saints is a restoration of the original Church established by Jesus Christ, which was built "upon the foundation of the apostles and prophets, Jesus Christ himself being the chief corner stone." It is not a breakoff from any other church.

We believe that the fulness of the gospel of Christ has been restored, but this is no reason for anyone to feel superior in any way toward others of God's children. Rather, it requires a greater obligation to invoke the essence of the gospel of Christ in our lives—to love, serve, and bless others."

~ *President James E. Faust   April 2006*

Experience:

"I take you back 184 years to the year 1823. The month was September—the night of September 21–22, to be exact.

The boy Joseph Smith had prayed that night before going to sleep. He asked the Lord for forgiveness of his light-mindedness. A miraculous thing then happened. He says:

"While I was thus in the act of calling upon God, I discovered a light appearing in my room, which continued to increase until the room was lighter than at noonday, when immediately a personage appeared at my bedside. ...

"He called me by name, and said unto me that he was a messenger sent from the presence of God ... and that his name was Moroni; that God had a work for me to do; and that my name should be had for good and evil among all nations, kindreds, and tongues, or that it should be both good and evil spoken of among all people" (Joseph Smith—History 1:30, 33).

The boy must have been stunned by what he heard. In the eyes of those who knew him, he was simply a poor, unlearned farm boy. He had no wealth. His neighbors were in the same condition. His parents were struggling farmers. The area where they lived was rural and largely unknown. They were simply ordinary people trying to survive through hard work.

And yet an angel of God said that Joseph's "name should be had for good and evil among all nations, kindreds, and tongues." How could it be? That description fits the entire world.

Now, as we look back 177 years to the organization of the Church, we marvel at what has already happened. When the Church was organized in 1830 there were but six members, only a handful of believers, all residing in a largely unknown village. Today, we have become the fourth or fifth largest church in North America, with congregations in every city of any consequence. Stakes of Zion today flourish in every state of the United States, in every province of Canada, in every state of Mexico, in every nation of Central America and throughout South America.

Congregations are found throughout the British Isles and Europe, where thousands have joined the Church through the years. This work has reached out to the Baltic nations and on down through Bulgaria and Albania and other areas of that part of the world. It reaches across the vast area of Russia. It reaches up into Mongolia and all down through the nations of Asia into the islands of the Pacific, Australia, and New Zealand, and into India and Indonesia. It is flourishing in many of the nations of Africa.

Our general conferences are carried by satellite and other means in 92 different languages.

And this is only the beginning. This work will continue to grow and prosper and move across the earth. It must do so if Moroni's promise to Joseph is to be fulfilled."

~ *President Gordon B. Hinckley   October 2007*

Scripture:

"Behold, because of their belief in me, saith the Father, and because of the unbelief of you, O house of Israel, in the latter day shall the truth come unto the Gentiles, that the fulness of these things shall be made known unto them."

~3 Nephi 16:7

Testimony:

"To you, this day, I affirm my witness of the calling of the Prophet Joseph, of his works, of the sealing of his testimony with his blood as a martyr to the eternal truth. Each of you can bear witness of the same thing. You and I are faced with the stark question of accepting the truth of the First Vision and that which followed it. On the question of its reality lies the very validity of this Church. If it is the truth, and I testify that it is, then the work in which we are engaged is the most important work on the earth.

I leave with you my testimony of the truth of these things, and I invoke the blessings of heaven upon you. May the windows of heaven be opened and blessings showered upon you as the Lord has promised. Never forget that this was His promise and that He has the power and the capacity to see that it is fulfilled. I so pray as I leave my blessing and love with you in the sacred name of our Redeemer, even the Lord Jesus Christ, amen."

~ President Gordon B. Hinckley   October 2007

Quest #66
Truth

Quote:

Then say, what is truth? 'Tis the last and the first,
For the limits of time it steps o'er.
Tho the heavens depart and the earth's fountains burst,
Truth, the sum of existence, will weather the worst,
Eternal, unchanged, evermore.
~*Oh Say, What Is Truth?* Hymn #272, verse 4

Experience:

"Several months ago I read the testimony of my great-grandfather's
sister Elizabeth Staheli Walker. As a child, Elizabeth immigrated to
America from Switzerland with her family.

After Elizabeth married, she and her husband and children lived in Utah
near the Nevada border, where they ran a mail station. Their home was a
stopping place for travelers. All day and all night they had to be ready to
cook and serve meals for travelers. It was hard, exhausting work, and they
had little rest. But the greatest thing that concerned Elizabeth was the
conversation of the people they associated with.

Elizabeth said that up to this time she had always taken for granted that
the Book of Mormon was true, that the Prophet Joseph Smith had been
authorized of God to do what he did, and that his message was the plan of
life and salvation. But the life she was experiencing was anything but what
would strengthen such a belief.

Some of the travelers who stopped were well-read, educated, smart
men, and always the talk around her table was that Joseph Smith was "a
sly fraud" who had written the Book of Mormon himself and then
distributed it to make money. They acted as if to think anything else was
absurd, claiming "that Mormonism was bunk."

All this talk made Elizabeth feel isolated and alone. There was no one to
talk to, no time to even say her prayers—although she did pray as she
worked. She was too frightened to say anything to those who ridiculed
her religion. She said she didn't know but what they were telling the
truth, and she felt she could not have defended her belief if she had tried.

Later, Elizabeth and her family moved. Elizabeth said she had more time
to think and was not so distracted all the time. She often went down in
the cellar and prayed to Heavenly Father about what was troubling her—

about the stories those seemingly smart men had told about the gospel being bunk and about Joseph Smith and the Book of Mormon.

One night Elizabeth had a dream. She said: "It seemed I was standing by a narrow wagon road, which led around by the foot of a low rolling hill; halfway up the hill I saw a man looking down and speaking, or seemed to be speaking, to a young man who was kneeling and leaning over a hole in the earth. His arms were stretched out, and it looked as if he was reaching for something from in the hole. I could see the lid of stone that seemed to have been taken off from the hole over which the boy was bending. On the road were many people, but none of them seemed to be at all interested in the two men on the hillside. There was something that came along with the dream that impressed me so strangely that I woke right up; … I could not tell my dream to anyone, but I seemed to be satisfied that it meant the angel Moroni [instructed] the boy Joseph at the time he got the plates."

In the spring of 1893, Elizabeth went to Salt Lake City to the dedication of the temple. She described her experience: "In there I saw the same picture [that] I had seen in my dream; I think it was [a] colored-glass window. I feel satisfied that if I saw the Hill Cumorah itself, it would not look more real. I feel satisfied that I was shown in a dream a picture of the angel Moroni giving Joseph Smith the [gold] plates."

Many years after having this dream and several months before she died at nearly age 88, Elizabeth received a powerful impression. She said, "The thought came to me as plain … as if someone had said to me, … 'Do not bury your testimony in the ground.'"
~ Cheryl A. Esplin   April 2015

Scripture:

"He that keepeth his commandments receiveth truth and light, until he is glorified in truth and knoweth all things."
~Doctrine and Covenants 93:28

Testimony:

"To be at peace in these wonderful yet challenging times, we must learn true doctrine, gain pure testimony, and live the truths of the gospel courageously. As we live in harmony with the light and truth taught by Jesus Christ and by His prophets, we will see more clearly our eternal destiny. I so testify in the name of Jesus Christ, amen."
~ Elder Robert R. Steuer   April 2008

Quest #67
Rescue

Quote:

"There is no greater work in all the world than that of saving souls. Incomparable joy can be yours when you bring souls unto Him!"
~*President Ezra Taft Benson   April 1983*

Experience:

"One Sunday morning some 30 years ago, while I was serving in a stake presidency, we received a telephone call from one of our faithful bishops. He explained that his ward had grown so rapidly that he could no longer provide a meaningful calling to all worthy members. His plea to us was that we divide the ward. While waiting for such approval, we decided as a stake presidency that we would visit the ward and call all these wonderful, worthy brothers and sisters to be stake missionaries.

About the third person I visited was a young female student attending the local university. After chatting for a few moments, I issued the call to serve as a missionary. There was silence for a few moments. Then she said, "President, don't you know that I am not active in the Church?"

After a few moments of silence on my part, I said, "No, I did not know you were not active."

She answered, "I have not been active in the Church for years." Then she said, "Don't you know that when you have been inactive, it's not all that easy to come back?"

I responded, "No. Your ward starts at 9:00 a.m. You come into the chapel, and you are with us."

She answered, "No, it is not that easy. You worry about a lot of things. You worry if someone will greet you or if you will sit alone and unnoticed during the meetings. And you worry about whether you will be accepted and who your new friends will be."

With tears rolling down her cheeks, she continued, "I know that my mother and father have been praying for me for years to bring me back into the Church." Then after a moment of silence, she said, "For the last three months I have been praying to find the courage, the strength, and the way to come back into activity." Then she asked, "President, do you suppose this calling could be an answer to those prayers?"

My eyes started to water as I responded, "I believe the Lord has answered your prayers."
~*Bishop Richard C. Edgley   April 2012*

Scripture:

"Remember the worth of souls is great in the sight of God;

And if it so be that you should labor all your days in crying repentance unto this people, and bring, save it be one soul unto me, how great shall be your joy with him in the kingdom of my Father!

And now, if your joy will be great with one soul that you have brought unto me into the kingdom of my Father, how great will be your joy if you should bring many souls unto me!"

~D & C 18: 10, 15-16

Testimony:

"I testify that you were called of God and you are sent to serve His children. He wants that no one be left behind. President Monson holds the keys of the priesthood in all the earth. God will give you inspiration and strength to meet your charge to help His children find their way to the happiness made possible by the Atonement of Jesus Christ. I so testify to you in the sacred name of Jesus Christ, amen."

~President Henry B. Eyring   April 2009

Quest #68
The Gospel of Jesus Christ

Quote:

"And there is no cure for the ills of the world except the gospel of the Lord Jesus Christ. Our hope for peace, for temporal and spiritual prosperity, and for an eventual inheritance in the kingdom of God is found only in and through the restored gospel. There is no work that any of us can engage in that is as important as preaching the gospel and building up the Church and kingdom of God on earth."

~ *President Joseph Fielding Smith   April 1972*

Experience:

"In later years I have reflected on the message the Savior taught the woman of Samaria.

"Jesus saith unto her, Give me to drink." The woman was amazed that he would talk to her. The Master said: "If thou knewest the gift of God, and who it is that saith to thee, Give me to drink; thou wouldest have asked of him, and he would have given thee living water." (John 4:7, 9–10.) It is evident that she was talking about well water and he was talking about "living water."

This difficulty of understanding about water recalls the story of a sailing ship that had become disabled in a storm. It drifted aimlessly for many days. The crew and passengers became famished and parched from lack of food and water. Finally another ship came into view. They signaled frantically for water. The other ship replied, "Let down your buckets where you are." This communication made no sense at all, for they supposed they were far out to sea in typical ocean water. Again the famished ones requested water. Again the signal came, "Let down your buckets where you are." They could not know that they had drifted into the mouth of a great river and that the water beneath them was fresh and could save their lives. The water of life lay just beneath them, yet they were dying for lack of this knowledge.

Like those passengers, multitudes of people are thirsting for "living water," and they know not where to find it. Like the people on the other ship, we are signaling that we have found the "living water." It has brought us the abundant life. It has made us happy, healthy, and serene. We who enjoy the abundant life want to share this happiness. You, too, may want to drink of this "living water."

~*A. Theodore Tuttle   April 1975*

Scripture:

"And even so I have sent mine everlasting covenant into the world, to be a light to the world, and to be a standard for my people, and for the Gentiles to seek to it, and to be a messenger before my face to prepare the way before me."
~D&C 45:9

And no unclean thing can enter into his kingdom; therefore nothing entereth into his rest save it be those who have washed their garments in my blood, because of their faith, and the repentance of all their sins, and their faithfulness unto the end.

Now this is the commandment: Repent, all ye ends of the earth, and come unto me and be baptized in my name, that ye may be sanctified by the reception of the Holy Ghost, that ye may stand spotless before me at the last day.

Verily, verily, I say unto you, this is my gospel; and ye know the things that ye must do in my church; for the works which ye have seen me do that shall ye also do; for that which ye have seen me do even that shall ye do;

Therefore, if ye do these things blessed are ye, for ye shall be lifted up at the last day.
~3 Nephi 27:19-22

Testimony:

"Now, my brethren, I want to leave with you my witness. I know that God lives, and I am striving with all my soul to know God himself. I do not remember the time when I had any question about the truths of the gospel of Jesus Christ. I know as I live that Jesus lives, that he was and is the Only Begotten Son of God in the flesh, and that he is our Redeemer.

I know that Joseph Smith opened this last dispensation. It is thrilling to me to contemplate the fact that the Father and the Son stood before Joseph in the grove and that the Father gave the Prophet a personal introduction to his Son, Jesus Christ, our Lord. I know that angels came and restored the priesthood to the Prophet and Oliver Cowdery; that God did establish again his church upon the earth; that The Church of Jesus Christ of Latter-day Saints is his church; that Jesus Christ is the only name given under heaven whereby men can be saved; that acceptance and obedience to the gospel of Jesus Christ, which we have the honor to preach and are commissioned to carry to all the ends of the earth, is the only means of salvation for this world, both temporally and spiritually.

I shall not know these things better in the not-too-distant future when I shall stand before the Lord to give an account of my work in mortality. As I bear you this testimony I pray that we shall all fully live the gospel and thereby qualify as true disciples of Christ, to obtain the promised peace in this world and eternal life in the world to come. This I do in the name of Jesus Christ. Amen."

~ President Marion G. Romney   October 1978

Quest #69
Teaching with the Spirit

Quote:

"While we are all teachers, we must fully realize that it is the Holy Ghost who is the real teacher and witness of all truth."

~ *Matthew O. Richardson   2nd Counselor in the Sunday School Presidency October 2011*

Experience:

"A traveller in the Eastern country overtook an old gentleman walking towards a town, and asked him, 'Who is the great man of that little town? Who is your leading man? Who is the governor and controlling spirit of that little place?' The old gentleman replied, 'I am the king of that little town.' 'Really,' says the traveller, 'are you the leading man?' 'Yes, sir, I am king in that place, and reign as king.' 'How do you make this to appear? Are you in affluent circumstances?' 'No, I am poor; but in that little village there are so many children. All those children go to my school; I rule the children, and they rule their parents, and that makes me king.'"

~*President Brigham Young   Journal of Discourses, 9:39.*

Scripture:

"And the Spirit shall be given unto you by the prayer of faith;
and if ye receive not the Spirit ye shall not teach."

~*D&C 42: 14*

Testimony:

"May I urge each member of the Church, when you are serving as a teacher, to remember that every human soul is precious to our Father in Heaven, for we are all his children. God's children are entitled to be taught the truths of the gospel in clear and understandable terms so that the Spirit can confirm the truths of the gospel to them.]

["To the master teacher, the Lord Jesus Christ, whose resurrection we celebrate at this Easter time, I say: I thank thee, oh Lord, for teaching us that there is no greater call than to be an effective teacher. In the name of Jesus Christ, amen."

~ *Elder M. Russel Ballard   April 1983*

Quest #70
Stand on Holy Ground

Quote:

"Thirty years' experience has taught me that every moment of my life must be holiness to the Lord, resulting from equity, justice, mercy and uprightness in all my actions, which is the only course by which I can preserve the Spirit of the Almighty to myself."

~*President Brigham Young   Deseret News, Apr. 2, 1862, 313.*

Experience:

"On December 26, 2004, a powerful earthquake struck off the coast of Indonesia, creating a deadly tsunami that killed more than 200,000 people. It was a terrible tragedy. In one day, millions of lives were forever changed.

But there was one group of people who, although their village was destroyed, did not suffer a single casualty.

The reason?

They knew a tsunami was coming.

The Moken people live in villages on islands off the coast of Thailand and Burma (Myanmar). A society of fishermen, their lives depend on the sea. For hundreds and perhaps thousands of years, their ancestors have studied the ocean, and they have passed their knowledge down from father to son.

One thing in particular they were careful to teach was what to do when the ocean receded. According to their traditions, when that happened, the "Laboon"—a wave that eats people—would arrive soon after.

When the elders of the village saw the dreaded signs, they shouted to everyone to run to high ground.

Not everyone listened.

One elderly fisherman said, "None of the kids believed me." In fact, his own daughter called him a liar. But the old fisherman would not relent until all had left the village and climbed to higher ground."

~*Elder Joseph B. Wirthlin   October 2005*

Scripture:

"Wherefore, stand ye in holy places, and be not moved, until the day of the Lord come;…"

~*D&C 87: 8*

Testimony:

"As President Brigham Young taught, "Every moment of [our lives] must be holiness to the Lord, … which is the only course by which [we] can preserve the Spirit of the Almighty to [ourselves]." May the Lord bless each and all of us in our special responsibility to find holiness to the Lord by standing in holy places. That is where we will find the spiritual protection we need for ourselves and our families. That is the source of help to carry forth the word of the Lord in our time. Standing in holy places will help us rise above the evil influences of our time and draw us closer to our Savior. I testify that if we do this, the Lord will bless us forever and we will be made mighty "in faith and in works."12 In the name of Jesus Christ, amen.

~ President James E. Faust   April 2005

Quest #71
America

Quote:

"Men may fail in this country, earthquakes may come, seas may heave beyond their bounds, there may be great drought, disaster, and hardship, but this nation, founded on principles laid down by men whom God raised up, will never fail. This is the cradle of humanity, where life on this earth began in the Garden of Eden. This is the place of the new Jerusalem. This is the place that the Lord said is favored above all other nations in all the world. This is the place where the Savior will come to His temple. This is the favored land in all the world. Yes, I repeat, men may fail, but this nation won't fail. I have faith in America; you and I must have faith in America, if we understand the teachings of the gospel of Jesus Christ. We are living in a day when we must pay heed to these challenges.

I plead with you not to preach pessimism. Preach that this is the greatest country in all the world. This is the favored land. This is the land of our forefathers. It is the nation that will stand despite whatever trials or crises it may yet have to pass through."

~President Harold B. Lee   "Ye Are the Light of the World", pp. 350-51

Experience:

"Yes, this is a land fertilized by the blood of patriots. During the struggle for independence, nearly 9,000 of the colonist forces were killed. Among those fifty-six patriots who had pledged their lives, their fortunes, and their sacred honor by signing the Declaration of Independence, at least nine paid that price with their life's blood.

At the close of the Revolution, the thirteen states found themselves independent but then faced grave internal economic and political problems. The Articles of Confederation had been adopted but proved to be ineffectual. Under this instrument, the nation was without a president, a head. There was a congress, but it was a body destitute of any power. There was no supreme court. The states were merely a confederation.

Washington wrote of the defects of this loose federation in these words: "The fabrick which took nine years, at the expense of much blood and treasure to rear, now totters to the foundation, and without support must soon fall." (John C. Fitzpatrick, ed., Writings of George Washington, Washington, D.C.: Government Printing Office, 1939, 29:68.) Because of this crisis, fifty-five of the seventy-four appointed delegates reported to the convention, representing every state except Rhode Island, for the purpose of forming "a more perfect union." Thirty-nine finally signed the Constitution.

Who were these delegates, those whom the Lord designated "wise men" whom he raised up? They were mostly young men in the prime of their life, their average age being forty-four. Benjamin Franklin was the eldest at eighty-one. George Washington, the presiding officer at the convention, was fifty-five. Alexander Hamilton was only thirty-two; James Madison, who recorded the proceedings of the convention with his remarkable Notes, was only thirty-six. These were young men, but men of exceptional character, "sober, seasoned, distinguished men of affairs, drawn from various walks of life." (J. Reuben Clark, Jr., Stand Fast by Our Constitution, Deseret Book Co., 1965, p. 135.)

Of the thirty-nine signers, twenty-one of them were educated in the leading American colleges and in Great Britain; eighteen were, or had been, lawyers or judges; twenty-six had seen service in the Continental Congress; nineteen had served in the Revolutionary army, seventeen as officers. Four had been on Washington's personal staff during the war. Among that assembly of the thirty-nine signers were to be found two future presidents of the United States, one the "Father of his Country"; a vice-president of the United States; a secretary of the treasury; a secretary of war; a secretary of state; two chief justices of the Supreme Court, and three who served as justices; and the venerable Franklin, a diplomat, philosopher, scientist, and statesman.

"They were not backwoodsmen from far-off frontiers, not one of them. ... There has not been another such group of men in all [the 200 years of our history] that even challenged the supremacy of this group." (J. Reuben Clark, Jr., Conference Reports, April 1957, p. 47.) President Wilford Woodruff said they "were the best spirits the God of heaven could find on the face of the earth. They were choice spirits. ..." (Wilford Woodruff, Cr, April 1898, p. 89; italics added.)

Following the drafting of the Constitution, it awaited ratification by the states. In 1787 three states ratified the Constitution. In the next year eight more followed; and on April 6, 1789, 187 years ago today, the Constitution of the United States went into operation as the basic law of the United States when the electoral college unanimously elected George Washington as the first president of the nation. This date, I believe, was not accidental.

In the final analysis, what the framers did, under the inspiration of God, was to draft a document that merited the approval of God himself, who

declared it to "be maintained for the rights and protection of all flesh."
(D&C 101:77; italics added.)
~President Ezra Taft Benson   April 1976

Scripture:

"And inasmuch as ye shall keep my commandments, ye shall prosper, and shall be led to a land of promise; yea, even a land which I have prepared for you; yea, a land which is choice above all other lands.
~1 Nephi 2:20

Testimony:

"I testify to you that God's hand has been in our destiny. I testify that freedom as we know it today is being threatened as never before in our history. I further witness that this land—the Americas—must be protected, its Constitution upheld, for this is a land foreordained to be the Zion of our God. He expects us as members of the Church and bearers of His priesthood to do all we can to preserve our liberty.

May God bless us that, with His help, we will not fail to bring to pass His purposes on earth. In the name of Jesus Christ, amen."
~ President Ezra Taft Benson   October 1979

Quest #72
Abide with Christ

Quote:

Abide with me; 'tis eventide,
And lone will be the night
If I cannot commune with thee
Nor find in thee my light.
The darkness of the world, I fear,
Would in my home abide.

O Savior, stay this night with me;
Behold, 'tis eventide.
O Savior, stay this night with me;
Behold, 'tis eventide.

~ *Lowrie M. Hofford*   *'Abide with Me; 'Tis Eventide' (Hymns #165, verse 3)*

Experience:

"That power will protect them when they go to places where they will
be the only Latter-day Saints. They will not be alone nor without strength,
because they accepted the invitation to gather with the Saints when it
was not easy.

That strength is given to those who are older as well as the young. I
know a widow more than 90 years of age. She is in a wheelchair. She
prays as you do, pleading for help to solve problems beyond her human
power to resolve. The answer is a feeling in her heart. It draws her to keep
a commandment: "And behold, ye shall meet together oft." So she finds a
way to get to her meetings. People who attend there have told me, "We
are so glad to see her. She brings such a spirit with her."

She partakes of the sacrament, and she renews a covenant. She
remembers the Savior, and she tries to keep His commandments. And so
she takes His Spirit with her, always. Her problems may not be resolved.
Most of them come from the choices of others, and even the Heavenly
Father who hears her prayers and loves her cannot force others to choose
the right. But He can send her to the safety of the Savior and the promise
of His Spirit to be with her. And so I am sure that she will, in the strength
of the Lord, pass the test she faces, because she keeps the commandment
to gather often with the Saints. That is both the evidence that she is
enduring well and the source of her strength for what lies ahead."

~*President Henry B. Eyring   April 2004*

Scripture:

"Abide in me, and I in you. As the branch cannot bear fruit of itself, except it abide in the vine; no more can ye, except ye abide in me."
~John 15:4

Testimony:

"Jesus said, "Without me ye can do nothing." I testify that that is God's truth. Christ is everything to us and we are to "abide" in Him permanently, unyieldingly, steadfastly, forever. For the fruit of the gospel to blossom and bless our lives, we must be firmly attached to Him, the Savior of us all, and to this His Church, which bears His holy name. He is the vine that is our true source of strength and the only source of eternal life. In Him we not only will endure but also will prevail and triumph in this holy cause that will never fail us. May we never fail it nor fail Him I pray in the sacred and holy name of Jesus Christ, amen.."

~ Elder Jeffrey R. Holland   April 2004

Quest #73
Atonement

Quote:
"Men cannot forgive their own sins; they cannot cleanse themselves from the consequences of their sins. Men can stop sinning and can do right in the future, and so far [as] their acts are acceptable before the Lord [become] worthy of consideration. But who shall repair the wrongs they have done to themselves and to others, which it seems impossible for them to repair themselves? By the atonement of Jesus Christ the sins of the repentant shall be washed away; though they be crimson they shall be made white as wool [see Isaiah 1:18]. This is the promise given to you."
~ President Joseph F. Smith   *Teachings of Presidents of the Church: Joseph F. Smith, 99–100*

Experience:
"On March 20, 1934, Howard and Claire Hunter's first child was born, a son they named Howard William Hunter Jr. and called Billy. During the summer they noticed that Billy seemed lethargic. Doctors diagnosed him with anemia, and Howard twice gave blood for transfusions, but Billy's condition did not improve. Further tests revealed a severe intestinal problem that was causing Billy to lose blood. Doctors performed surgery, with Howard lying beside his son to give blood, but the results were not encouraging. Three days later, on October 11, 1934, little Billy died quietly as his parents sat beside his bed. "We were grief-stricken and numb as we left the hospital into the night," Howard wrote.

Through the experiences of Billy's death and the deaths of other loved ones, President Hunter was sustained by his testimony of the Savior's Atonement and Resurrection. "It is our firm belief that [the Atonement] is a reality," he testified, "and nothing is more important in the entire divine plan of salvation than the atoning sacrifice of Jesus Christ. We believe that salvation comes because of the atonement. In its absence the whole plan of creation would come to naught. ... Without this atoning sacrifice, temporal death would be the end, and there would be no resurrection and no purpose in our spiritual lives. There would be no hope of eternal life."
~President Howard W. Hunter   *Teachings of Presidents of the Church: Howard W. Hunter, 99-101*

Scripture:
"For as in Adam all die, even so in Christ shall all be made alive."
~1 Corinthians 15:22

Testimony:

"Everything worthy and eternal is centered in the living reality of God, our loving Eternal Father, and His Son, Jesus Christ, and His Atonement, witnessed by the Holy Ghost.9 This is Easter Sunday. I reverently witness and solemnly testify of the living Christ—He who "died, was buried, and rose again the third day, and ascended into heaven." He is Alpha and Omega—with us in the beginning, He is with us to the end."

~Elder Gerrit W. Gong   April 2018

Quest #74
The Second Coming

Quote:

"Most people have the wrong idea of what is meant by the end of the world. …

"…When Christ comes there will be an end to the world. … There will not be any war, any turmoil, envying, lying; there will be no wickedness. Men will learn then to love the Lord and keep His commandments, and if they don't they will not stay here. That's the end of the world, and that is what the Savior prayed for when His disciples came to Him and said, 'Teach us to pray.' What did He do? He taught them, 'Our Father who art in Heaven, hallowed be Thy name, Thy kingdom come, Thy will be done in earth as it is in heaven.' [See Luke 11:1–2.]

"That's what I'm praying for. The Lord was praying for the end of the world, and so am I."

~ *President Joseph Fielding Smith*   *The Signs of the Times (1943), 103–5.*

Experience:

"Three beautiful examples of the Lord's hand in establishing His kingdom are the temples announced today by President Monson. Only a few decades ago, who could have imagined temples in Haiti, Thailand, and the Ivory Coast?

The location of a temple is not a convenient geographical decision. It comes by revelation from the Lord to His prophet, signifying a great work to be done and acknowledging the righteousness of the Saints who will treasure and care for His house through generations. …

…Who could imagine a house of the Lord in the beautiful city of Bangkok? Christians are only 1 percent of this principally Buddhist country. As in Haiti we also find in Bangkok that the Lord has gathered the elect of the earth. While there a few months ago, we met Sathit and Juthamas Kaivaivatana and their devoted children. Sathit joined the Church when he was 17 and served a mission in his native land. Later he met Juthamas at the institute, and they were sealed in the Manila Philippines Temple. In 1993 the Kaivaivatanas were hit by a truck whose driver had fallen asleep, and Sathit was paralyzed from his chest down. Their faith has never wavered. Sathit is an admired teacher at the International School Bangkok.   He serves as the stake president of the Thailand Bangkok North Stake. We see God's miracles in His wondrous work and in our own personal lives. …

…God's miracles are not happening just in Haiti, Thailand, or the Ivory Coast. Look around you. "God is mindful of every people … ; yea, he numbereth his people, and his … mercy [is] over all the earth."…

…Our faith grows as we anticipate the glorious day of the Savior's return to the earth. The thought of His coming stirs my soul. It will be breathtaking! The scope and grandeur, the vastness and magnificence, will exceed anything mortal eyes have ever seen or experienced."
~Elder Neil L. Andersen   April 2015

Scripture:

This know also, that in the last days perilous times shall come.

For men shall be lovers of their own selves, covetous, boasters, proud, blasphemers, disobedient to parents, unthankful, unholy,

Without natural affection, trucebreakers, false accusers, incontinent, fierce, despisers of those that are good,

Traitors, heady, highminded, lovers of pleasures more than lovers of God;

Having a form of godliness, but denying the power thereof: from such turn away.

For of this sort are they which creep into houses, and lead captive silly women laden with sins, led away with divers lusts,

Ever learning, and never able to come to the knowledge of the truth.
~ 2 Timothy 3:1-7

Testimony:

"The time will come when every knee will bow, and every tongue confess to and acknowledge him, and when they who have lived upon the earth and have spurned the idea of a Supreme Being and of revelations from him, will fall with shamefacedness and humble themselves before him, exclaiming, "There is a God! O God, we once rejected thee and disbelieved thy word and set at naught thy counsels, but now we bow down in shame and we do acknowledge that there is a God, and that Jesus is the Christ." This time will come, most assuredly. We have the faith of the Gospel of the Lord Jesus.
~President Brigham Young   Discourses of Brigham Young, 112-13

Quest #75
Building Personal Testimony

Quote:

"To persevere firm and steadfast in the faith of Christ requires that the gospel of Jesus Christ penetrate one's heart and soul, meaning that the gospel becomes not just one of many influences in a person's life but the defining focus of his or her life and character."

~Elder D. Todd Christofferson

Experience:

"Lorenzo Snow was baptized and confirmed in June 1836. Recalling his developing testimony, he later said: "I believed they [the Latter-day Saints] had the true religion, and I joined the Church. So far my conversion was merely a matter of reason."

"I was perfectly satisfied that I had done what was wisdom for me to do under the circumstances."

"I had had no manifestation, but I expected one."

"This manifestation did not immediately follow my baptism, as I expected," he recalled. "But, although the time was deferred, when I did receive it, its realization was more perfect, tangible and miraculous than even my strongest hopes had led me to anticipate. One day while engaged in my studies, some two or three weeks after I was baptized, I began to reflect upon the fact that I had not obtained a knowledge of the truth of the work—that I had not realized the fulfillment of the promise: 'He that doeth my will shall know of the doctrine;' [see John 7:17] and I began to feel very uneasy.

I laid aside my books, left the house and wandered around through the fields under the oppressive influence of a gloomy, disconsolate spirit, while an indescribable cloud of darkness seemed to envelop me. I had been accustomed, at the close of the day, to retire for secret prayer to a grove, a short distance from my lodgings, but at this time I felt no inclination to do so.

The spirit of prayer had departed, and the heavens seemed like brass over my head. At length, realizing that the usual time had come for secret prayer, I concluded I would not forego my evening service, and, as a matter of formality, knelt as I was in the habit of doing, and in my accustomed retired place, but not feeling as I was wont to feel.

I had no sooner opened my lips in an effort to pray, than I heard a sound, just above my head, like the rustling of silken robes, and immediately the Spirit of God descended upon me, completely enveloping my whole person, filling me from the crown of my head to the soles of my feet, and O, the joy and happiness I felt! No language can describe the instantaneous transition from a dense cloud of mental and spiritual darkness into a refulgence of light and knowledge, as it was at that time imparted to my understanding. I then received a perfect knowledge that God lives, that Jesus Christ is the Son of God, and of the restoration of the Holy Priesthood, and the fulness of the gospel.

It was a complete baptism—a tangible immersion in the heavenly principle or element, the Holy Ghost; and even more real and physical in its effects upon every part of my system than the immersion by water; dispelling forever, so long as reason and memory last, all possibility of doubt or fear in relation to the fact handed down to us historically, that the 'Babe of Bethlehem' is truly the Son of God; also the fact that He is now being revealed to the children of men, and communicating knowledge, the same as in the apostolic times. I was perfectly satisfied, as well I might be, for my expectations were more than realized, I think I may safely say, in an infinite degree.

I cannot tell how long I remained in the full flow of this blissful enjoyment and divine enlightenment, but it was several minutes before the celestial element, which filled and surrounded me, began gradually to withdraw. On arising from my kneeling posture, with my heart swelling with gratitude to God beyond the power of expression, I felt—I knew that he had conferred on me what only an Omnipotent Being can confer—that which is of greater value than all the wealth and honors worlds can bestow."

~ President Lorenzo Snow   Teachings of Presidents of the Church: Lorenzo Snow, 59-62

Scripture:

"Nevertheless, ye are blessed, for the testimony which ye have borne is recorded in heaven for the angels to look upon; and they rejoice over you, and your sins are forgiven you."

~Doctrine and Covenants 62: 3

"If thou shalt ask, thou shalt receive revelation upon revelation, knowledge upon knowledge, that thou mayest know the mysteries and peaceable things—that which bringeth joy, that which bringeth life eternal."

~Doctrine and Covenants 42: 61

Testimony:

"I know it is true." Because those few words have been said a billion times by millions of people does not make it trite. It will never be worn out. I feel sorry for people who try to couch it in other words, because there are no words like "I know." There are no words which express the deep feelings which can come from the human heart like "I know."

Some of our good people get so terrified at triteness that they try to steer around and away from their testimonies by getting out on the fringes. Don't you ever worry about triteness in testimony. When the President of the Church bears his testimony, he says, "I know that Joseph Smith was called of God, a divine representative. I know that Jesus is the Christ, the Son of the living God." You see, the same thing every one of you says. That is a testimony. It never gets old, never gets old! Tell the Lord frequently how much you love him."

~President Spenser W. Kimball   The Teachings of Spencer W. Kimball, ed. Edward L. Kimball (1982), 141, New Era, Aug. 1981, 6.

Quest #76
Unity

Quote:

"Girls and boys, young women and young men, sisters and brothers, we are on this journey together. In order to reach our sublime destiny, we need each other, and we need to be unified. The Lord has commanded us, "Be one; and if ye are not one ye are not mine."
~Reyna I. Aburto; Second Counselor in the Relief Society General Presidency   April 2018

"Nay, speak no ill; a kindly word
Can never leave a sting behind;
And, oh, to breathe each tale we've heard
Is far beneath a noble mind.
Full oft a better seed is sown
By choosing thus the kinder plan,
For, if but little good is known,
Still let us speak the best we can.

"Then speak no ill, but lenient be
To other's failings as your own.
If you're the first a fault to see,
Be not the first to make it known,
For life is but a passing day;
No lip may tell how brief its span;
Then, O the little time we stay,
Let's speak of all the best we can."
Anon.   Nay, Speak No Ill (Hymns, no. 233)

Experience:

"On 9 April 1951, five days after President Smith's death, Latter-day Saints met for general conference and sustained President David O. McKay as President of the Church. There they learned that President Clark, who had served faithfully as first counselor for almost 17 years, had been called to serve as second counselor. President Stephen L. Richards had been called as first counselor.

Sensing that Church members would question this change, President McKay took time in general conference to explain the calling of his two counselors. He said that President Richards had been called as first counselor because he had served longer than President Clark in the apostleship. Emphasizing that this practice was not an "established policy," President McKay simply said that "it seemed advisable" in the callings of Presidents Richards and Clark.

As President McKay continued with his address, he spoke of the unity he felt with his counselors: "We do not want any member in this Church, nor any man or woman listening in to harbor the thought for a moment that there has been any rift between the two counselors who sustained President Smith in the Quorum of the First Presidency, and President Grant for the years that we were together with that inspired leader. Neither should you feel that there is any demotion. President Clark is a wonderful servant. ...

"You should understand further, that in the counselorship of the Quorum of the First Presidency these two men are coordinate in authority, in love, and confidence, in freedom to make suggestions, and recommendations, and in their responsibility not only to the Quorum but also to the Lord Jesus Christ and to the people generally.

"They are two great men. I love them both, and say God bless them, and give you the assurance that there will be harmony and love and confidence in the Quorum of the First Presidency as you have sustained them today."

~President David O. McKay   April 1951(Teachings of Presidents of the Church, David O. McKay,39-40)

Scripture:

"...I say unto you, be one; and if ye are not one ye are not mine."

~*Doctrine and Covenants 38: 27*

"And he commanded them that there should be no contention one with another, but that they should look forward with one eye, having one faith and one baptism, having their hearts knit together in unity and in love one towards another."

~*Mosiah 18: 21*

Testimony:

"I bear you my solemn witness that the unity we now experience will increase. God the Father lives. He hears and answers our prayers in love. The Savior Jesus Christ, resurrected and glorious, lives and reaches out to us in mercy. This is His true Church. President Monson is the living prophet of God. If we are united in sustaining him with all our hearts, with willing obedience to do what God would have us do, we will move

together in power to go wherever God would have us go and to become what He wants us to be."
~*President Henry B. Eyring   October 2008*

Quest #77
Firm in the Faith

Quote:

"And so it is. Each of us will be greatly blessed if we know the stories of faith and sacrifice that led our forefathers to join the Lord's Church.

From the first time Robert and Maria heard Wilford Woodruff teach and testify of the Restoration of the gospel, they knew the gospel was true.

They also knew that no matter what trials or hardships would come to them, they would be blessed for staying true to the faith. It almost seems that they had heard the words of our prophet today, who said, "No sacrifice is too great … in order to receive [the] blessings [of the temple]" (Thomas S. Monson, "The Holy Temple—a Beacon to the World," Ensign or Liahona, May 2011, 92)."
~Elder William R. Walker   April 2014

Experience:

"John Taylor firmly believed that the kingdom of God would be established on earth. He understood that this effort was not dependent on the Prophet Joseph Smith or any other man, but that it was ultimately directed by the Lord. And he was ready to defend this effort with his life.

In 1838, soon after his call to the Quorum of the Twelve, John Taylor traveled toward Far West, Missouri, to join the Saints. Along the way, he was scheduled to speak to a group near Columbus, Ohio.   A little before the appointed time, some brethren brought news that a number of men had gathered at the meeting place and were plotting to tar and feather Elder Taylor. The brethren advised him to cancel the meeting because they were outnumbered and would not be able to protect him. However, Elder Taylor insisted he would go and preach as planned and would do so even if he had to go by himself.

When he reached the large crowd assembled to hear him, he proceeded to speak first about his having recently come from countries ruled by monarchs. He told them about the honor he felt of standing on free soil. In reference to how that freedom was achieved, he said: "Gentlemen, I now stand among men whose fathers fought for and obtained one of the greatest blessings ever conferred upon the human family⊡—the right to think, to speak, to write; the right to say who shall govern them, and the right to worship God according to the dictates of their own consciences⊡—all of them sacred, human rights, and now guaranteed by the American Constitution. I see around me the sons of those noble sires, who, rather than bow to the behests of a tyrant, pledged their lives, fortunes and sacred honors to burst those fetters, enjoy freedom themselves, bequeath it to their posterity, or die in the attempt."

Elder Taylor then continued: "But, by the by, I have been informed that you purpose to tar and feather me, for my religious opinions. Is this the boon you have inherited from your fathers? Is this the blessing they purchased with their dearest hearts' blood⬚—this your liberty? If so, you now have a victim, and we will have an offering to the goddess of liberty."

Having said that, he tore open his vest and exclaimed: "Gentlemen come on with your tar and feathers, your victim is ready; and ye shades of the venerable patriots, gaze upon the deeds of your degenerate sons! Come on, gentlemen! Come on, I say, I am ready!" Elder Taylor paused for a few minutes, but no one would move or speak. He then continued his remarks and preached to the crowd with boldness and power for three hours.

Even in the face of opposition, John Taylor testified boldly of the truth and worked tirelessly for the establishment of the kingdom of God.

As Elder Matthias F. Cowley of the Quorum of the Twelve said many years later after the death of President Taylor, "He lived, labored and died the perfect exemplification of his favored motto, 'The Kingdom of God or nothing.'"
~ *President John Taylor   Teachings of the Presidents of the Church: John Taylor, 219-221*

Scripture:

"Nevertheless they did fast and pray oft, and did wax stronger and stronger in their humility, and firmer and firmer in the faith of Christ, unto the filling their souls with joy and consolation, yea, even to the purifying and the sanctification of their hearts, which sanctification cometh because of their yielding their hearts unto God."
~*Helaman 3:35*

Testimony:

"Always remember the promise of good things to come, both now and hereafter, for those who are firm and steadfast in the faith of Christ. Remember "eternal life, and the joy of the saints." "O all ye that are pure in heart, lift up your heads and receive the pleasing word of God, and feast upon his love; for ye may, if your minds are firm, forever." In the name of Jesus Christ, amen."
~*Elder D. Todd Christofferson   October 2018*

Quest #78
Christ's Church Restored

Quote:
"This year we are commemorating the 200th anniversary of the birth of the Prophet Joseph Smith. To the world we testify that he was the prophet of God foreordained to bring about the Restoration of the gospel of Jesus Christ. This he did under the direction of our Savior, …"

I acknowledge the Lord's hand in the Restoration of the gospel. Through the inspired sacrifices of God's children through the ages, the foundation of the Restoration was laid, and the world is preparing for the Second Coming of our Lord and Savior Jesus Christ."
~Elder Robert D. Hales   October 2005

Experience:
"Some years ago I was assigned to the Rochester New York Stake conference. On Saturday I said to the brethren who were with me, 'Let us get up early in the morning, early Sunday morning, and go to the Sacred Grove before the conference.' They all agreed. Accordingly, very early on that spring Sabbath, the mission president, the stake president, the regional representative, and I went out to Palmyra and walked into the grove. No one else was there. It was peaceful and beautiful. It had rained during the night. Tiny new leaves were upon the trees.

"We spoke quietly one to another. We knelt upon the damp ground and prayed. We did not hear an audible voice. We did not see a vision. But in an indefinable way we were told in our minds, each of us, that yes, it happened here just as Joseph said it happened. It was here that God our Eternal Father and His Beloved Son, the resurrected Lord Jesus Christ, appeared to the 14-year-old boy and spoke with him. Their matchless light rested upon him, and he was instructed in what he should do.

"That sublime occasion, the First Vision, parted the curtains through which came the restoration to earth of the Church of Christ. It came out of the wilderness of darkness, out of the bleakness of ages past into the glorious dawn of a new day. The Book of Mormon followed as another witness of the Lord Jesus Christ. His holy supernal priesthood was restored under the hands of those who held it anciently. Keys and powers were bestowed upon the Prophet and his associates. The ancient Church was again upon the earth with all of the blessings, powers, doctrines, keys, and principles of previous dispensations. It is [Christ's] Church. It carries His name. It is governed by His priesthood. There is no other name under heaven by which men must be saved. Joseph Smith … became His great testator."

~ *President Gordon B. Hinckley   First Presidency Christmas Devotional December 3, 2000*

Scripture:

And are built upon the foundation of the apostles and prophets, Jesus Christ himself being the chief corner stone;

~Ephesians 2:20

Testimony:

"We leave with you our testimony of the divinity of this work. What a wonderful work it is. How empty our lives would be without it. God our Eternal Father lives. He loves us. He watches over us. Jesus is the Christ, the Redeemer of mankind. They have restored Their work in this last and final dispensation through the instrumentality of the Prophet Joseph. I so testify in all solemnity and leave my love and my blessing with you, my beloved brethren and sisters of this grateful Church. God bless you every one."

~President Gordon B. Hinckley   October 2005

Quest #79
Strengthened by the Lord

Quote:

"For some reason, we think the Atonement of Christ applies only at the end of mortal life to redemption from the Fall, from spiritual death. It is much more than that. It is an ever-present power to call upon in everyday life. When we are racked or harrowed up or tormented by guilt or burdened with grief, He can heal us. While we do not fully understand how the Atonement of Christ was made, we can experience 'the peace of God, which passeth all understanding'"
~President Boyd K. Packer   April 2001

Experience:

"...I would like to share the story of Susanna Stone Lloyd, who at the age of 26 left England in 1856 and traveled to Utah alone. The only member of her family to join the Church, Susanna was a member of the Willie Handcart Company. Like so many other pioneers, she endured life-threatening hunger, illness, and fatigue.

Upon arriving in the Salt Lake Valley, Susanna borrowed a mirror to make herself more presentable. Despite her best efforts, she recounts: "I shall never forget how I looked. Some of my old friends did not know me." Having sold her own mirror to an Indian for a piece of buffalo meat, she had not spent much time looking at herself. Now she did not recognize her own image. She was a different person, both inside and out. Over the course of rocky ridges and extreme hardship came a deep conviction. Her faith had been tried, and her conversion was concrete. She had been refined in ways that the very best mirror could not reflect. Susanna had prayed for strength and found it—deep within her soul."
~ Ellen W. Smoot   April 2002

Scripture:

""Fear thou not; for I am with thee: be not dismayed; for I am thy God: I will strengthen thee; yea, I will help thee"
~Isaiah 41:10
"I can do all things through Christ which strengtheneth me"
~Philippians 4:13

Testimony:

"One day all of these mortal burdens will pass away and there will be no more pain (see Revelation 21:4). I pray that we will all understand the

hope and strength of our Savior's Atonement: the assurance of immortality, the opportunity for eternal life, and the sustaining strength we can receive if only we will ask, in the name of Jesus Christ, amen."
~*Elder Dallin H. Oaks*   October 2015

Quest #80
Representing Christ

Quote:
"Christ says 'Give me All. I don't want so much of your time and so much of your money and so much of your work: I want You.'"
~C. S. Lewis, Mere Christianity (1960), 153.

Experience:
"We recently held an open house in the Arizona Temple. Following a complete renovation of that building, nearly a quarter of a million people saw its beautiful interior. On the first day of the opening, clergymen of other religions were invited as special guests, and hundreds responded. It was my privilege to speak to them and to answer their questions at the conclusion of their tours. I told them that we would be pleased to answer any queries they might have. Many were asked. Among these was one which came from a Protestant minister.

Said he: "I've been all through this building, this temple which carries on its face the name of Jesus Christ, but nowhere have I seen any representation of the cross, the symbol of Christianity. I have noted your buildings elsewhere and likewise find an absence of the cross. Why is this when you say you believe in Jesus Christ?"

I responded: "I do not wish to give offense to any of my Christian brethren who use the cross on the steeples of their cathedrals and at the altars of their chapels, who wear it on their vestments, and imprint it on their books and other literature. But for us, the cross is the symbol of the dying Christ, while our message is a declaration of the living Christ."

He then asked: "If you do not use the cross, what is the symbol of your religion?"

I replied that the lives of our people must become the only meaningful expression of our faith and, in fact, therefore, the symbol of our worship."
~ Elder Gordon B. Hinckley   April 1975

Scripture:
"For I am not ashamed of the gospel of Christ: for it is the power of God unto salvation to every one that believeth; to the Jew first, and also to the Greek."
~Romans 1:16

Testimony:
"I bear my solemn witness to you that there is one true shepherd—our Lord Jesus Christ—one faith, one baptism, and only one church of Christ. I urge all who listen to the voice of the Good Shepherd to investigate the

message of His church today and gain a personal witness of its truthfulness. I humbly bear my testimony to the truthfulness of these things and beseech all of you to gain that personal witness, and do so in the name of Jesus Christ. Amen.

~Elder Delbert L. Stapley April 1977

Quest #81
Remember the Sabbath

Quote:

"Our observance or nonobservance of the Sabbath is an unerring measure of our attitude toward the Lord personally and toward his suffering in Gethsemane, his death on the cross, and his resurrection from the dead. It is a sign of whether we are Christians in very deed, or whether our conversion is so shallow that commemoration of his atoning sacrifice means little or nothing to us."
~*Elder Mark E. Petersen   April 1975*

Experience:

"I met a great little family some time ago while attending a stake conference. They bore a sweet testimony to me of what the sacrament has come to mean to them. The father some years before had lost his job when a factory he had been working in had closed. Rather than move to another city to obtain new employment, he proposed that the family open a family fast- food business. The business was successful for several years; then a chain fast-food business opened up across the street and remained open seven days a week. In family council they determined that they must meet the competition. They would remain open on Sunday and take turns going to Church. After one year of seven-days-a-week operation, they discovered they were worn out, cross with each other, and complained about every little thing that would arise.

Another family council was called and the proposition presented that they close on Sunday to see if they could get back their family spirit. They soon discovered that the Lord's system works. Even though sales were fewer, profits increased."
~Elder L. Tom Perry   October 1984

Scripture:

"Remember the sabbath day to keep it holy.

"Six days shalt thou labour, and do all thy work:

"But the seventh day is the sabbath of the Lord thy God: in it thou shalt not do any work, thou, nor thy son, nor thy daughter, thy manservant, nor thy maidservant, nor thy cattle, nor thy stranger that is within thy gates:

"For in six days the Lord made heaven and earth, the sea, and all that in them is, and rested the seventh day: wherefore the Lord blessed the sabbath day, and hallowed it."
~Exodus 20:8–11

<u>Testimony:</u>

"From the scriptures, let us remember, "The sabbath was made for man, and not man for the sabbath." (Mark 2:27.) And again He has instructed us in the Doctrine and Covenants, "Trifle not with sacred things." (D&C 6:12.)

I give you my witness that the greatest joy you can experience here in mortality is being obedient to the will of the Lord. May we always strive to keep His commandments, and may we keep His sacred day holy is my prayer, in the name of Jesus Christ, amen."

~Elder L. Tom Perry   October 1984

Quest #82
Easter

Quote:

"The reality of the Resurrection of the Savior overwhelms our heartbreak with hope because with it comes the assurance that all the other promises of the gospel are just as real—promises that are no less miraculous than the Resurrection. We know that He has the power to cleanse us from all our sins. We know that He has taken upon Himself all our infirmities, pains, and the injustices we have suffered. We know that He has "rise[n] from the dead, with healing in his wings." We know that He can make us whole no matter what is broken in us. We know that He "shall wipe away all tears from [our] eyes; and there shall be no more death, neither sorrow, nor crying, neither shall there be any more pain." We know that we can be "made perfect through Jesus … , who wrought out this perfect atonement," if we will just have faith and follow Him."
~Elder Paul V. Johnson   April 2016

Experience:

"To find the most important day in history, we must go back to that evening almost 2,000 years ago in the Garden of Gethsemane when Jesus Christ knelt in intense prayer and offered Himself as a ransom for our sins. It was during this great and infinite sacrifice of unparalleled suffering in both body and spirit that Jesus Christ, even God, bled at every pore. Out of perfect love, He gave all that we might receive all. His supernal sacrifice, difficult to comprehend, to be felt only with all our heart and mind, reminds us of the universal debt of gratitude we owe Christ for His divine gift.

Later that night, Jesus was brought before religious and political authorities who mocked Him, beat Him, and sentenced Him to a shameful death. He hung in agony upon the cross until, finally, "it [was] finished." His lifeless body was laid in a borrowed tomb. And then, on the morning of the third day, Jesus Christ, the Son of Almighty God, emerged from the tomb as a glorious, resurrected being of splendor, light, and majesty."
~ Elder Dieter F. Uchtdorf   April 2018

Scripture:

"Behold, I am Jesus Christ, whom the prophets testified shall come into the world.

And behold, I am the light and the life of the world; and I have drunk out of that bitter cup which the Father hath given me, and have glorified the

Father in taking upon me the sins of the world, in the which I have suffered the will of the Father in all things from the beginning.

And it came to pass that the multitude went forth, and thrust their hands into his side, and did feel the prints of the nails in his hands and in his feet; and this they did do, going forth one by one until they had all gone forth, and did see with their eyes and did feel with their hands, and did know of a surety and did bear record, that it was he, of whom it was written by the prophets, that should come.

And when they had all gone forth and had witnessed for themselves, they did cry out with one accord, saying:

Hosanna! Blessed be the name of the Most High God! And they did fall down at the feet of Jesus, and did worship him."
~3 Nephi 11:10-11, 15-17

Testimony:

"My beloved brothers and sisters, I testify that the most important day in the history of mankind was the day when Jesus Christ, the living Son of God, won the victory over death and sin for all of God's children. And the most important day in your life and mine is the day when we learn to "behold the man"; when we see Him for who He truly is; when we partake with all our heart and mind of His atoning power; when with renewed enthusiasm and strength, we commit to follow Him. May that be a day that recurs over and over again throughout our lives.

I leave you my testimony and blessing that as we "behold the man," we will find meaning, joy, and peace in this earthly life and eternal life in the world to come. In the sacred name of Jesus Christ, amen."
~ Elder Dieter F. Uchtdorf   April 2018

Quest #83
Come unto Christ

Quote:
"To all within the sound of my voice, the voice of Christ comes ringing down through the halls of time, asking each one of us while there is time, "Do you love me?" And for every one of us, I answer with my honor and my soul, "Yea, Lord, we do love thee." And having set our "hand to the plough," we will never look back until this work is finished and love of God and neighbor rules the world."
~Elder Jeffrey R. Holland   October 2012

Experience:
"A certain man went down from Jerusalem to Jericho, and fell among thieves, which stripped him of his raiment, and wounded him, and departed, leaving him half dead.

"And by chance there came down a certain priest that way: and when he saw him, he passed by on the other side.

"And likewise a Levite, when he was at the place, came and looked on him, and passed by on the other side.

"But a certain Samaritan, as he journeyed, came where he was: and when he saw him, he had compassion on him,

"And went to him, and bound up his wounds, pouring in oil and wine, and set him on his own beast, and brought him to an inn, and took care of him.

"And on the morrow when he departed, he took out two pence, and gave them to the host, and said unto him, Take care of him; and whatsoever thou spendest more, when I come again, I will repay thee".

Then Jesus asked the lawyer, "Which now of these three, thinkest thou, was neighbour unto him that fell among the thieves?"
~ Luke 10:30-36

Scripture:
"And now, my beloved brethren, I would that ye should come unto Christ, who is the Holy One of Israel, and partake of his salvation, and the power of his redemption. Yea, come unto him, and offer your whole souls as an offering unto him, and continue in fasting and praying, and endure to the end; and as the Lord liveth ye will be saved."
~Omni 1:26

Testimony:

"I testify that we are happier when we follow the teachings of the gospel of Jesus Christ. As we strive to follow Him, the blessings of heaven will come unto us. I know His promises will be fulfilled as we make and keep covenants and become true followers of Christ. I testify of His great love for each one of us, and I do so in the name of Jesus Christ, amen."
~ *Elder Walter F. González   April 2011*

Quest #84
Look to God and Live

Quote:

In golden youth when seems the earth
A summer-land of singing mirth,
When souls are glad and hearts are light,
And not a shadow lurks in sight,
We do not know it, but there lies
Somewhere veiled 'neath evening skies
A garden which we all must see—
The garden of Gethsemane. ...

Down shadowy lanes, across strange streams
Bridged over by our broken dreams;
Behind the misty caps of years,
Beyond the great salt fount of tears,
The garden lies. Strive, as you may,
You cannot miss it in your way.
All paths that have been, or shall be
Pass somewhere through Gethsemane.
~Ella Wheeler Wilcox, "Gethsemane," in Sourcebook of Poetry, comp. Al Bryant (1968), 435.

Experience:

"Last week I received a faith-filled letter from Laurence M. Hilton. May I share with you the account of surviving personal tragedy with faith, nothing wavering.

In 1892, Thomas and Sarah Hilton, Laurence's grandparents, went to Samoa, where Thomas was set apart as mission president after their arrival. They brought with them a baby daughter; two sons were born to them while they served there. Tragically, all three died in Samoa, and in 1895 the Hiltons returned from their mission childless.

David O. McKay was a friend of the family and was deeply touched by their loss. In 1921, as part of a world tour of visits to the members of the Church in many nations, Elder McKay stopped in Samoa, accompanied by Elder Hugh J. Cannon. Before leaving on his tour, he had promised the now-widowed Sister Hilton that he would personally visit the graves of her three children. I share with you the letter David O. McKay wrote to her from Samoa:

"Dear Sister Hilton:

"Just as the descending rays of the late afternoon sun touched the tops of the tall coconut trees, Wednesday, May 18th, 1921, a party of five stood with bowed heads in front of the little Fagali'i Cemetery. … We were there, as you will remember, in response to a promise I made you before I left home.

"The graves and headstones are in a good state of preservation. … I reproduce here a copy I made as I stood … outside the stone wall surrounding the spot.

"Janette Hilton
Bn: Sept. 10, 1891
Died: June 4, 1892
'Rest, darling Jennie'

"George Emmett Hilton
Bn: Oct. 12, 1894
Died: Oct. 19, 1894
'Peaceful be thy slumber'

"Thomas Harold Hilton
Bn: Sept. 21, 1892
Died: March 17, 1894
'Rest on the hillside, rest'

"As I looked at those three little graves, I tried to imagine the scenes through which you passed during your young motherhood here in old Samoa. As I did so, the little headstones became monuments not only to the little babes sleeping beneath them, but also to a mother's faith and devotion to the eternal principles of truth and life. Your three little ones, Sister Hilton, in silence most eloquent and effective, have continued to carry on your noble missionary work begun nearly 30 years ago, and they will continue as long as there are gentle hands to care for their last earthly resting place.

By loving hands their dying eyes were closed;
By loving hands their little limbs composed;
By foreign hands their humble graves adorned;
By strangers honored, and by strangers mourned.

"Tofa Soifua,

"David O. McKay"

~*President Thomas S. Monson   April 1998*

Scripture:

"For I know that my redeemer liveth, and that he shall stand at the latter day upon the earth:

And though after my skin worms destroy this body, yet in my flesh shall I see God:

Whom I shall see for myself, and mine eyes shall behold,..."

~Job 19: 25-27

Testimony:

"With all my heart and the fervency of my soul, I lift up my voice in testimony as a special witness and declare that God does live. Jesus is His Son, the Only Begotten of the Father in the flesh. He is our Redeemer; He is our Mediator with the Father. He it was who died on the cross to atone for our sins. He became the firstfruits of the Resurrection. Because He died, all shall live again. "Oh, sweet the joy this sentence gives: 'I know that my Redeemer lives!'" May the whole world know it and live by that knowledge, I humbly pray, in the name of Jesus Christ, the Lord and Savior, amen."

~President Thomas S. Monson   April 2007

Quest #85
Sacrament

Quote:

"The ordinance of the sacrament is a holy and repeated invitation to repent sincerely and to be renewed spiritually. The act of partaking of the sacrament, in and of itself, does not remit sins. But as we prepare conscientiously and participate in this holy ordinance with a broken heart and a contrite spirit, then the promise is that we may always have the Spirit of the Lord to be with us. And by the sanctifying power of the Holy Ghost as our constant companion, we can always retain a remission of our sins."

~*Elder David A. Bednar   April 2016*

Experience:

"A Young Women leader recently learned about the strength we receive as we strive to thoughtfully partake of the sacrament. Working to complete a requirement in Personal Progress, she set a goal to focus on the words in the sacrament hymns and prayers.

Each week, she conducted a self-evaluation during the sacrament. She recalled mistakes she had made, and she committed to be better the next week. She was grateful to be able to make things right and be made clean. Looking back on the experience, she said, "I was acting on the repentance part of the Atonement."

One Sunday after her self-evaluation, she began to feel gloomy and pessimistic. She could see that she was making the same errors over and over again, week to week. But then she had a distinct impression that she was neglecting a big part of the Atonement—Christ's enabling power. She was forgetting all the times the Savior helped her be who she needed to be and serve beyond her own capacity.

With this in mind, she reflected again on the previous week. She said: "A feeling of joy broke through my melancholy as I noted that He had given me many opportunities and abilities. I noted with gratitude the ability I had to recognize my child's need when it wasn't obvious. I noted that on a day when I felt I could not pack in one more thing to do, I was able to offer strengthening words to a friend. I had shown patience in a circumstance that usually elicited the opposite from me."

She concluded: "As I thanked God for the Savior's enabling power in my life, I felt so much more optimistic toward the repentance process I was working through and I looked to the next week with renewed hope."

~ *Cheryl A. Esplin   October 2014*

Scripture:

"For behold, I, God, have suffered these things for all, that they might not suffer if they would repent;

But if they would not repent they must suffer even as I;

Which suffering caused myself, even God, the greatest of all, to tremble because of pain, and to bleed at every pore, and to suffer both body and spirit—and would that I might not drink the bitter cup, and shrink—

Nevertheless, glory be to the Father, and I partook and finished my preparations unto the children of men."

~Doctrine and Covenants 19: 16-19

Testimony:

"Beloved friends, as we unite across the globe each week in what we hope is an increasingly sacred acknowledgment of Christ's majestic atoning gift to all humankind, may we bring to the sacramental altar "more tears for his sorrows [and] more pain at his grief." And then, as we reflect, pray, and covenant anew, may we take from that sacred moment "more patience in suff'ring, … more praise for relief." For such patience and relief, for such holiness and hope, I pray for all of you in the name of Him who broke the precious bread of forgiveness and poured the holy wine of redemption, even Jesus Christ, the great and merciful and holy Lamb of God, amen."

~ Elder Jeffrey R. Holland   April 2019

Quest #86
Feast on the Words

Quote:

"Once we understand why we need guidance and where we obtain it, we then ask, how can we achieve it? How can we truly live, not "by bread alone, but by every word that proceedeth out of the mouth of God"?

We begin with a determination to "liken all scriptures unto us … for our profit and learning." If we "press forward, feasting upon the word of Christ, and endure to the end, … [we] shall have eternal life."

To feast means more than to taste. To feast means to savor. We savor the scriptures by studying them in a spirit of delightful discovery and faithful obedience. When we feast upon the words of Christ, they are embedded "in fleshy tables of the heart." They become an integral part of our nature."

~*President Russell M. Nelson   October 2000*

Experience:

"Two years ago, the Lord touched my dear mother's heart, which helped her decide to receive the ordinance of baptism. I had waited for that day to take place for almost 35 years. In order for her to make that decision, many members of the Church truly ministered to her as Christ would. One Sunday, she felt she should go to church. She followed the prompting. While she sat on the front row and waited for the sacrament service to begin, a four-year-old boy stood in front of her and looked at her. She greeted him with a smile. The little boy left her presence abruptly and walked back to his own seat, which was on the other side of the row where my mother was seated. This little boy picked up something from his seat and came back and handed my mother a hymnbook and walked back to his seat. My mother noticed a hymnbook was placed on every other chair in the chapel. She could have easily picked one up from the chair next to her. However, she was very impressed with the boy's innocent act of kindness, which he had learned in his home and at church. It was a tender moment for her. She had a strong impression that God was inviting her to come and follow the Savior. She felt she should be baptized. This little boy did not seek recognition for what he did, but he simply did his best to live the word of God and to love his neighbor. His kindness created an important change of heart in my mother.

The words of Christ will profoundly touch hearts and open the eyes of those who do not yet see Him. On the road to Emmaus, two disciples walked with Jesus. They were sad and did not comprehend that the Savior had triumphed over death. In their grief, they did not recognize that the living Christ was walking with them. Though Jesus "expounded unto them in all the scriptures the things concerning himself," they still did not recognize Him as the resurrected Savior until they sat and broke bread with Him. Then did their "eyes" open. As we—or our friends, associates, and neighbors—feast and break bread with Him, our eyes of understanding will open. When the disciples at Emmaus reflected on their time with the resurrected Savior, they said that their hearts burned within them while He opened the scriptures to them (see Luke 24:27–32). This will be true for all of us."

~ *Elder Takashi Wada of the Seventy   April 2019*

Scripture:

"Angels speak by the power of the Holy Ghost; wherefore, they speak the words of Christ. Wherefore, I said unto you, feast upon the words of Christ; for behold, the words of Christ will tell you all things what ye should do.

~*2 Nephi 32: 3*

Testimony:

"Oh, my brethren, let us not treat lightly the great things we have received from the hand of the Lord! His word is one of the most valuable gifts He has given us. I urge you to recommit yourselves to a study of the scriptures. Immerse yourselves in them daily so you will have the power of the Spirit to attend you in your callings. Read them in your families and teach your children to love and treasure them. Then prayerfully and in counsel with others, seek every way possible to encourage the members of the Church to follow your example. If you do so, you will find, as Alma did, that "the word [has] a great tendency to lead people to do that which [is] just—yea, it [has] more powerful effect upon the minds of the people than the sword, or anything else, which [has] happened unto them." (Alma 31:5.)

Like Alma, I say unto you, "It [is] expedient that [you] should try the virtues of the word of God" (Alma 31:5), in the name of Jesus Christ, amen."

~ *President Ezra Taft Benson   April 1986*

Quest #87
Live Holy Lives

Quote:

""And so I beg of you … to live each day so that you might receive from the fountain of light [the] nourishment and strength sufficient to every day's need. Take time to be holy each day of your lives."
~President Harold B. Lee   Decisions For Successful Living (1973), 149-50

Experience:

"Years ago, my adventurous son Jeff and I found ourselves on an old bus bouncing along on a dirt road in Central America at 1:00 A.M. We took the early, early bus because it was the only bus that day. A half hour later, the driver stopped for two missionaries. When they got on, we asked them where in the world they were going so early. Zone conference! And they were determined to do whatever it took to get there. At 2:00 A.M. two more elders boarded the bus and enthusiastically hugged their fellow missionaries. This scene repeated itself every half hour as the bus climbed the remote mountain road. By 5:00 A.M. we had 16 of the Lord's finest as fellow passengers and were basking in the Spirit they brought on board.

Suddenly, we screeched to a halt. A massive mud slide had buried the road. Jeff said, "What do we do now, Dad?" Our friends Stan, Eric, and Allan had the same concern. Just then, the zone leader shouted, "Let's go, elders. Nothing is going to stop us!" And they scrambled off the bus! We looked at each other and said, "Follow the elders," and we all sloshed through the mud slide, trying to keep up with the missionaries. There happened to be a truck on the other side, so we all hopped aboard. After a mile, we were stopped by yet another mud slide. Once again the elders plowed through, with the rest of us close behind. But this time there was no truck. Boldly, the zone leader said, "We will be where we are supposed to be even if we have to walk the rest of the way." Years later, Jeff told me how those missionaries and this photo inspired and motivated him tremendously as he served the Lord in Argentina.

Although we overcame the mud slides, we were all spotted with mud. The missionaries were somewhat nervous about standing before their president on zone conference day when he and his wife would be carefully checking their appearance.

As you and I slosh through the mud slides of life, we can't help getting a few mud spots on us along the way either. And we don't want to stand before the Lord looking muddy.

When the Savior appeared in ancient America, He said, "Repent, all ye ends of the earth, and come unto me and be baptized in my name, that ye may be sanctified by the reception of the Holy Ghost, that ye may stand spotless before me at the last day" (3 Ne. 27:20).

Alma warns us about some of the ways we become spotted with mud: "For our words will condemn us, yea, all our works will condemn us; we shall not be found spotless; and our thoughts will also condemn us" (Alma 12:14).

Alma also said:

"Ye cannot be saved; for there can no man be saved except his garments are washed white; yea, his garments must be purified until they are cleansed from all stain. ..."

~Elder Clate W. Mask Jr. of the Seventy   April 2004

Scripture:

"Have ye walked, keeping yourselves blameless before God? Could ye say, if ye were called to die at this time, within yourselves, that ye have been sufficiently humble? That your garments have been cleansed and made white through the blood of Christ, who will come to redeem his people from their sins?"

~Alma 5: 27

Testimony:

"I pray that the Lord may say of us, as Alma said of his son Shiblon: "And now, my son, I trust that I shall have great joy in you, because of your steadiness and your faithfulness unto God; for as you have commenced in your youth to look to the Lord your God, even so I hope that you will continue in keeping his commandments; for blessed is he that endureth to the end" (Alma 38:2).

I bear testimony that in time and in eternity God will bless our steadiness as we invite his children to come unto Christ. In the name of Jesus Christ, amen."

~ President Henry B. Eyring   April 1988

Quest #88
Agency and Acountability

Quote:

"It is our privilege to determine our own exaltation or degradation; it is our privilege to determine our own happiness or misery in the world to come."

~ *President John Taylor   Deseret News (Weekly), 9 Jan. 1861, 353.*

Experience:

"As a young man I served a mission to Brazil. It was a marvelous experience. One of the wonders of the world in that great country is Iguaçu Falls. In the flood season, the volume of water spilling over the brink is the largest in the world. Every few minutes, millions of gallons of water cascade into the chasm below. One part of the falls, where the deluge is the heaviest, is called the Devil's Throat.

There are some large rocks standing just above, before the water rushes down into Devil's Throat. Years ago, reckless boatmen would take passengers in canoes to stand on those rocks and look down into the Devil's Throat. The water above the falls is usually calm and slow moving, and the atmosphere tranquil. Only the roar of the water below forewarns of the danger lurking just a few feet away. A sudden, unexpected current could take a canoe into the rushing waters, over the cliff, and down into the Devil's Throat. Those foolish enough to leave the canoes to stand on these treacherous wet rocks could so easily lose their footing and be swept away into the swirling currents below.

I recognize that some of you think of yourselves as daredevils, ready to take on almost any challenge. But some of these excursions for excitement will inevitably take you down into the Devil's Throat. The only safe course is to stay well away from the dangers of the Devil's Throat. President George Albert Smith strongly cautioned, "If you cross to the devil's side of the line one inch, you are in the tempter's power, and if he is successful, you will not be able to think or even reason properly, because you will have lost the spirit of the Lord."

~*President James E. Faust   April 2003*

Scripture:

"And now my beloved brethren, I have said these things unto you that I might awaken you to a sense of your duty to God, that ye may walk blameless before him, that ye may walk after the holy order of God, after which ye have been received."

~*Alma 7:22*

Testimony:

"My beloved brothers and sisters, don't walk! Run! Run to receive the blessings of agency by following the Holy Ghost and exercising the freedoms God has given us to do His will.

I bear my special witness on this special Easter day that Jesus Christ used His agency to do our Father's will.

Of our Savior, we sing, "His precious blood he freely spilt; His life he freely gave." And because He did, we have the priceless opportunity "to choose liberty and eternal life" through the power and blessings of His Atonement. May we freely choose to follow Him today and always, I pray in His holy name, even Jesus Christ, amen."

~Elder Robert D. Hales   April 2015

Quest #89
Character

Quote:

"We become what we want to be by consistently being what we want to become each day. Righteous character is a precious manifestation of what you are becoming. Righteous character is more valuable than any material object you own, any knowledge you have gained through study, or any goals you have attained no matter how well lauded by mankind. In the next life your righteous character will be evaluated to assess how well you used the privilege of mortality."
~ Elder Richard G. Scott   October 2010

"We sow our thoughts, and we reap our actions; we sow our actions, and we reap our habits; we sow our habits, and we reap our characters; we sow our characters, and we reap our destiny."
~C. A. Hall   The Home Book of Quotations, New York: Dodd, Mead & Company, 1935, p. 845

Experience:

"A group of religion instructors [were] taking a summer course on the life of the Savior and focusing particularly on the parables.

"When the final exam time came, ... the students arrived at the classroom to find a note that the exam would be given in another building across campus. Moreover, the note said, it must be finished within the two-hour time period that was starting almost at that moment.

"The students hurried across campus. On the way they passed a little girl crying over a flat tire on her new bike. An old man hobbled painfully toward the library with a cane in one hand, spilling books from a stack he was trying to manage with the other. On a bench by the union building sat a shabbily dressed, bearded man [in obvious distress].

"Rushing into the other classroom, the students were met by the professor, who announced they had all flunked the final exam.

"The only true test of whether they understood the Savior's life and teaching, he said, was how they treated people in need.

"Their weeks of study at the feet of a capable professor had taught them a great deal of what Christ had said and done." In their haste to finish the technicalities of the course, however, they failed to recognize the application represented by the three scenes that had been deliberately staged. They learned the letter but not the spirit. Their neglect of the little girl and the two men showed that the profound message of the course had not entered into their inward parts.

We must at times search our own souls and discover what we really are. Our real character, much as we would wish, cannot be hidden."
~President James E. Faust   April 1998

Scripture:

"Let thy bowels also be full of charity towards all men, and to the household of faith, and let virtue garnish thy thoughts unceasingly; then shall thy confidence wax strong in the presence of God; and the doctrine of the priesthood shall distil upon thy soul as the dews from heaven."
~ D&C 121:45

Testimony:

"I testify and declare that our Heavenly Father expects His children to exercise integrity, civility, fidelity, charity, generosity, morality, and all the "ity" virtues. May we have the humility to take the opportunity to act upon our responsibility to demonstrate our ability to do so, I pray in the sacred name of Jesus Christ, amen."
~Bishop H. David Burton   October 2009

Quest #90
Finding Joy

Quote:

"Let us relish life as we live it, find joy in the journey, and share our love with friends and family."

~ *President Thomas S. Monson* *October 2008*

Experience:

"Recently I stood on the north shore of a beautiful Pacific island gazing out to sea at daybreak. I was fascinated by the regularity with which the gigantic waves consistently moved forward to break on the shoreline. It reminded me of the constancy of the plan of the Lord, with its fixed, eternal law, and the security of enduring justice and the tenderness of mercy when earned by obedience. I noticed that each wave would crest at a different point on the horizon to find its unique path to shore. Some cascaded over rocks, leaving rivulets of foaming, white water. Others burst on the shore in individual patterns. They slid up the moistened sand with playful frothy edges, then bubbled and swirled as they receded.

I thought of the unending variety of possibilities the Lord has provided for us. We have so much freedom, so many opportunities to develop our unique personalities and talents, our individual memories, our personalized contributions. Since there would be no further opportunity to observe the majestic sea, I tried to imagine the glorious panorama the brilliant sun would later create. As I watched this magnificent scene in reverence, a window formed in the clouds; the glistening rays of the rising sun broke through the overcast sky, transforming everything with its luminescence, its color, its life. It was as if the Lord wanted to share an additional blessing, a symbol of the light of His teachings that gives brilliance and hope to everyone it touches. Tears of gratitude formed for this wondrous world in which we live, for the extraordinary beauty our Heavenly Father so freely shares with all who are willing to see. Truly, life is beautiful.

Do you take time to discover each day how beautiful your life can be? How long has it been since you watched the sun set? The departing rays kissing the clouds, trees, hills, and lowlands good night, sometimes tranquilly, sometimes with exuberant bursts of color and form."

~*Elder Richard G. Scott*   *April 1996*

Scripture:

"Adam fell that men might be; and men are, that they might have joy."

~ *2 Nephi 2:25*

Testimony:

"Heed these words of the Psalmist: "I have set the Lord always before me: because he is at my right hand, I shall not be moved. ... In [His] presence is fulness of joy." As this principle is embedded in our hearts, each and every day can be a day of joy and gladness. I so testify in the sacred name of Jesus Christ, amen.

~ President Russell M. Nelson   October 2016

Reader,

So, you got to the end of my book. I hope that you enjoyed it and that it was useful to you!

I would just like to thank you for giving me your valuable time. I am truly blessed to have such a fulfilling occupation, but I only have that job because of people like you; people kind enough to give my books a chance and to spend their hard-earned money buying them. For that I am eternally grateful.

If you would like to find out more about my other books, then please visit my website for full details. You can find them at:

www.questcheney.com

Also feel free to contact me on Facebook, Twitter, Goodreads, or email (all of the details are available on the website), as I would love to hear from you.

LEAVE ME A REVIEW

If you enjoyed this book and would like to help, then you could think about leaving a review on Amazon, Goodreads, or anywhere else that readers visit. The most important part of how well a book sells is how many positive reviews it has, so if you leave me one then you are directly helping me to continue on my journey as a writer.

THANK YOU!

Thanks in advance to everyone who does this. It means a lot. I appreciate all of you who read my books and especially those who review them.

SIGN UP FOR MORE

If you would like more information about my books, or would like to be notified when my new books are being released,

SIGN UP ON MY WEBSITE

www.questcheney.com

About the Author

Jeff Cheney has worked as a civilian contract mechanic for the US Army, a heavy equipment mechanic, a High School teacher, and currently works in high technology computer chip manufacturing. He has been writing science fiction and fantasy stories for enjoyment for over thirty-five years and has published five SF novels with his brothers, as well as two QuEST books of Quotes.

 He enjoys coaching youth basketball, working on cars and doing woodworking when the time allows. He has three grown children and lives in a small town in NW Oregon with his wife of 32 years.

Jeff has served in a multitude of callings in the Church of Jesus Christ of Latter-day Saints over the years; as a missionary in Guayaquil, Ecuador as a young man, and many others as the years have gone by.

www.ingramcontent.com/pod-product-compliance
Lightning Source LLC
Chambersburg PA
CBHW071847020426
42331CB00007B/1894